PROFESSOR RAMAN PRINJA

WONDERS of the NIGHT SKY

ASTRONOMY STARTS WITH JUST LOOKING UP

ILLUSTRATED BY **JAN BIELECKI**

ALADDIN
New York London Toronto Sydney New Delhi

BEYOND WORDS
Portland, Oregon

To Kamini, Vikas and Sachin – R. P.

For Inessa – J. B.

ALADDIN
An imprint of Simon & Schuster
Children's Publishing Division
1230 Avenue of the Americas
New York, NY 10020

BEYOND WORDS
1750 S.W. Skyline Blvd., Suite 20
Portland, Oregon 97221-2543
503-531-8700 / 503-531-8773 fax
www.beyondword.com

This Beyond Words/Aladdin edition May 2023
Text and illustrations copyright © 2022 by Hodder & Stoughton

Originally published in 2022 in Great Britain by Hachette Children's Group
Hardcover ISBN: 978-1-58270-877-5

For information about special discounts for bulk purchases, please contact
Simon & Schuster Special Sales at 1-866-506-1949 or business@simonandschuster.com.

The Simon & Schuster Speakers Bureau can bring authors to your live event.
For more information or to book an event contact the Simon & Schuster Speakers Bureau at 1-866-248-3049
or visit our website at www.simonspeakers.com.

Editors: Grace Glendinning, Melanie Palmer
Designer: Claire Jones
Illustrations: Jan Bielecki
Consultancy provided by Dhara Patel of Royal Observatory Greenwich, London, UK
The text of this book was set in Museo

Manufactured in China 0222 SCP

10 9 8 7 6 5 4 3 2 1

Library of Congress Control Number: 2021953074

The website addresses (URLs) included in this book were valid at the time of going to press. However, it is possible
that contents or addresses may have changed since the publication of this book. No responsibility for any such
changes can be accepted by either the author or the Publisher.

CONTENTS

FOREWORD

It is only within the last century that we have been able to explore space thanks to advanced computing and robotic spacecraft. And with the invention of the telescope dating back just over 400 years, the foundation of our understanding of the Universe has come from generations of people over millennia, simply looking up at the night sky, trying to make sense of the spectacles above them.

They saw bright, twinkling points of light and curtains of color in the atmosphere as well as distant, fuzzy patches and a cloudy band arching across the sky. Our ancestors were fascinated by the countless treasures of the Universe on display. Even though these early sky-watchers couldn't reach out and touch what they could see, their curiosity led them to explore further.

Astronomy has not only improved our understanding of the make-up and dynamics of our Universe, it has helped us reflect upon ourselves and our planet—a tiny speck in the endless cosmos. Astronomy and space exploration have pushed technology to the limits, yet for all that we have discovered, there is so much more we have left to learn.

And that is the beauty of it! Astronomy is a never-ending source of inspiration and scientific endeavor that should be made accessible to all, something Raman Prinja has advocated for tirelessly for many years. Royal Observatory Greenwich strives to engage and communicate astronomy with audiences young and old, to spark the flame of intrigue buried within us all.

We are proud to partner with Raman and Wayland on this striking publication, as part of our mutual aim to advance young people's understanding of the Universe. For nearly 350 years the Observatory has played a significant role in the history of astronomy and navigation, and with Raman's personal contribution to this field, we are so pleased to inspire the next generation together.

DHARA PATEL
Senior Manager of Astronomy Education,
Royal Observatory Greenwich, London, UK

ROYAL
OBSERVATORY
GREENWICH

PREPARING FOR THE NIGHT SKY

The night sky is a fascinating and beautiful place to explore. Using just your eyes, there are countless wonders of the Universe to pick out. This book will take you to the stars, planets, Moon, and comets. During these explorations you will come to understand what you are looking at and its place in the Universe. The most important thing when viewing the night sky is to have fun!

Let's start with a few handy tips on how best to go stargazing.

High and dark

When exploring the night sky, it helps to go to a dark site, far from streetlights and building lights (otherwise known as "light pollution"). To see as much of the sky as possible, it also helps to go somewhere high, such as a hill in an open park or field. Always make sure you are safe and with a trusted adult.

Give your eyes a chance

Our eyes are not used to seeing in the dark. They can take up to 30 minutes to fully adjust to darkness and pick out faint stars in the sky. If you need a light to see something while you stargaze (such as this book!), use a flashlight that has been dulled with a covering of red cellophane. Red light does not have the same glaring effect on our eyes as blue or white light.

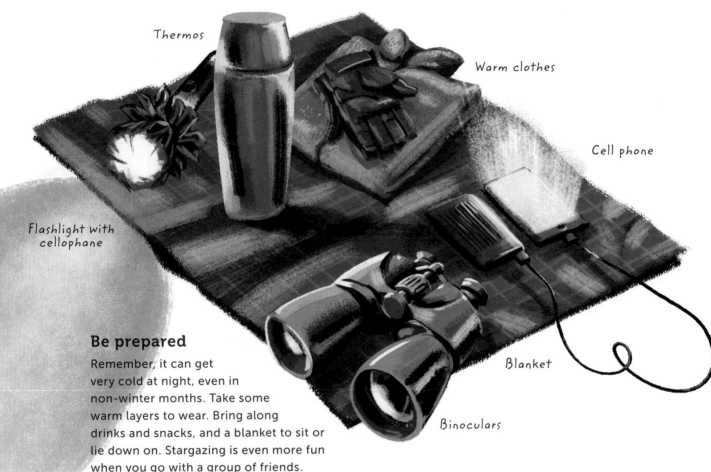

Thermos

Warm clothes

Cell phone

Flashlight with cellophane

Blanket

Binoculars

Be prepared

Remember, it can get very cold at night, even in non-winter months. Take some warm layers to wear. Bring along drinks and snacks, and a blanket to sit or lie down on. Stargazing is even more fun when you go with a group of friends.

A better look?

If you want a closer look at the planets, or craters on the Moon, binoculars are a great first tool to use. They are cheaper to buy and easier to carry around than a telescope. There are also many useful apps for a cell phone or tablet that can help you see the positions of stars from your location. Remember to use the red-light mode or night mode on your device.

Be patient

Astronomy requires patience and calm. The weather can suddenly turn cloudy and wet and your plans are ruined! Objects such as meteors may take hours to appear, and when one finally arrives you could miss it as it streaks across the sky. Most of the time you will be busy trying to find objects in the sky that are small and faint—think of it as an interstellar treasure hunt.

VARIETY OF STARS

On any clear night, you can *always* see stars in the sky. Depending on whether you live in a bright city or the dark countryside, there may be 100 to 2,000 stars on view every night.

*B*ut the stars are not all the same, so here are a few things to look out for:

Explore colors

Look carefully and you should notice that the stars are not all the same color. Some stars have an orange-red color, while others are blue-white or yellow-white.

KNOW WHY:

Stars have different colors because their surface temperatures are not all the same. Blue-white stars are hotter than yellow-white ones, which in turn are hotter than orange-red stars.

Explore brightness

Another thing to note is that the stars are not all the same brightness. Some stars are very faint, while others are much brighter.

KNOW WHY:

Some stars can be fainter because they are much farther away than others. Some stars also appear brighter because they are much larger and so are more powerful than smaller, cooler stars.

Explore specks

Notice how all the stars look like pinpricks in the night sky. Yet each one of these tiny, twinkling jewels is a vast, hot ball of glowing gas!

KNOW WHY:

Stars can be 10 times smaller and all the way up to 2,000 times bigger than the size of our Sun. These enormous objects appear so tiny in the sky because they are so far away from us.

The next nearest star to us after the Sun is called Proxima Centauri and it is 268,000 times farther from Earth than the Sun.

In a very dark sky, your eyes alone can see stars that are up to 93 million billion miles away!

CONSTELLATIONS
OF THE NORTHERN HEMISPHERE

A constellation is a group of stars that appear to form a shape. It's like a dot-to-dot puzzle in the sky! Most of the shapes were imagined thousands of years ago, by Greek and Roman poets, farmers, and astronomers, to tell stories about gods, legends, and amazing creatures.

Today, the International Astronomical Union has agreed on 88 constellations above us. If you get to know them, constellations can help you find your way around the night sky. Here are some that are most easily spotted from the northern hemisphere (the area of Earth above the equator).

Ursa Major

Ursa Major (also known as the Great Bear) is one of the most well-known constellations. To find it, look toward the northeast, between January and March from around 8:00 PM.

Within Ursa Major, also look out for the seven stars that make up a famous pattern called the Big Dipper.

Eta Ursae Minoris

Zeta Ursae Minoris

Pherkad

Kochab

POLARIS

Ursa Minor

Alkaid

Mizar

THE BIG DIPPER

Alioth

Megrez

Phecda

Dubhe

Merak

Ursa Major

Ursa Minor

You can use the Big Dipper's two brightest stars to hop over to another well-known constellation called Ursa Minor (or Little Bear). Polaris (or North Star) is the brightest star in Ursa Minor.

Cassiopeia

From April to June, look north after around 10:00 PM and try to pick out a *W*-shaped constellation called Cassiopeia, made up of five stars.

In Greek mythology, Queen Cassiopeia was chained to her throne in the sky for being too boastful!

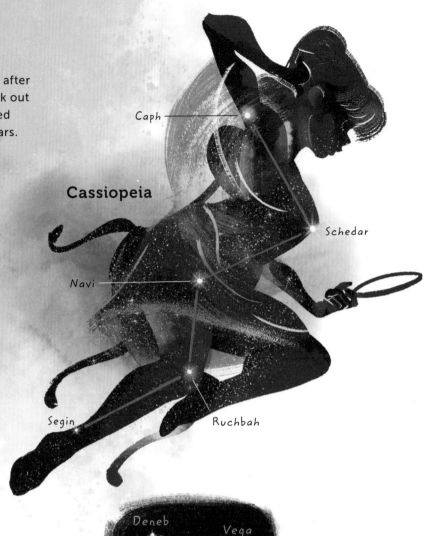

Cassiopeia

Caph

Schedar

Navi

Segin

Ruchbah

The Dumbbell Nebula

The stars you see in the night sky are not all the same age. Some are newly born, others may be halfway through their billions-of-years-long life cycle. The Dumbbell Nebula, or M27, is an example of a cloud of dust and gas blown off by a star that died at least 3,000 years ago.

On a clear, dark night, first look out for the Summer Triangle constellation—three bright stars high overhead in the northern hemisphere summer sky: Vega, Deneb, and Altair. Imagine lines connecting the stars in a triangle. The Dumbbell Nebula is about a third of the way up the line from Altair to Deneb.

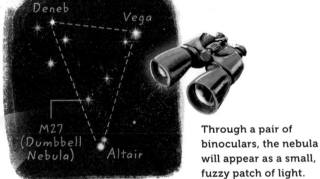

Deneb

Vega

M27 (Dumbbell Nebula)

Altair

Through a pair of binoculars, the nebula will appear as a small, fuzzy patch of light.

Viewed through a small telescope, you can start to see its shape and color. Look out for the double lobes that give the nebula its name.

Using a very powerful telescope like the Hubble Space Telescope, or 8-meter-wide telescopes on Earth used by astronomers, the beautiful details of the Dumbbell Nebula are revealed. This amazing sight is more than 1,200 light-years away from us.

ORION CLOSE-UP

Let's take a closer look at one of the greatest winter constellations in the northern hemisphere sky, called Orion (the Hunter). It is packed with some amazing details.

In Greek mythology, Orion was a talented hunter. He boasted to the gods that he could rid the Earth of all wild animals.

Orion the Hunter

Tabit

Bellatrix

Meissa

Betelgeuse

Betelgeuse

Betelgeuse

This is the second-brightest star in Orion and it marks the Hunter's right shoulder. Also known as Alpha Orionis, Betelgeuse is a red supergiant star. This massive star has a diameter at least 760 times wider than the Sun. Astronomers believe Betelgeuse will end its life in a supernova explosion.

The sword

Below Orion's belt there is an almost vertical, short line of bright points that represent the sword.

Rigel

Rigel is the bright, blue-white star that marks the Hunter's left leg. Also known as Beta Orionis, it is more than 800 light-years away from Earth. Rigel is 20 times more massive than the Sun, and is so powerful that it puts out more than 100,000 times more light energy than the Sun every second.

ORION'S BELT
Mintaka
Alnilam
Alnitak

THE SWORD
42 Orionis
Orion Nebula
Iota Orionis

Rigel

Saiph

Orion Nebula

Toward the middle of Orion's sword is a spectacular object known as the Orion Nebula. Though it's only seen as a fuzzy white blob through binoculars, powerful telescopes reveal it as a beautiful and colorful cloud of gas and dust that is 30–40 light-years from end to end.

Orion's belt

The belt of the Hunter is marked by three bright stars named Alnitak, Alnilam, and Mintaka. Alnitak and Mintaka, are really star systems made up of at least three stars each.

Orion Nebula close-up

The Orion Nebula is a giant star-making factory. Newborn stars are found there, and there is enough gas and dust in the nebula to give birth to thousands of new stars.

CONSTELLATIONS
OF THE SOUTHERN HEMISPHERE

If you live south of the equator, you are in the southern hemisphere and there are some fascinating constellations best viewed from there. Here are some examples to explore in the southern night skies.

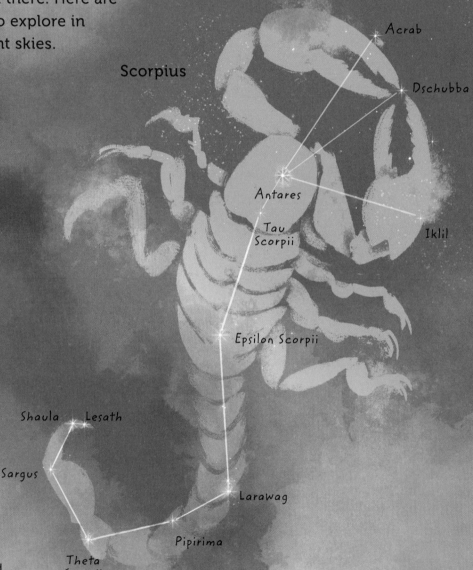

Scorpius

Acrab

Dschubba

Antares

Iklil

Tau Scorpii

Epsilon Scorpii

Shaula   Lesath

Sargus

Larawag

Pipirima

Theta Scorpii

Scorpius

Scorpius is a bright and big constellation that can be seen in southern skies between March and October. The name is the Latin for scorpion. The brightest star you can see in Scorpius is called Antares. It is classed as a red supergiant, more than 400 times larger in diameter than the Sun.

In Greek mythology, Scorpius was sent to destroy Orion, after the great hunter started to boast about his powers and began killing all the animals on Earth.

Centaurus

Centaurus is one of the largest constellations in the night sky. In Greek mythology it represents the centaur, a creature that is half-man and half-horse. It is clearly on view between March and mid-July in the southern skies. Centaurus includes two of the top 15 brightest stars in the sky, known as Alpha Centauri and Beta Centauri.

Omega Centauri is a sparkling collection of 10 million stars, held together in an object known as a globular cluster. The cluster lies about 16,000 light-years from Earth and contains tightly packed stars that are up to 12 billion years old.

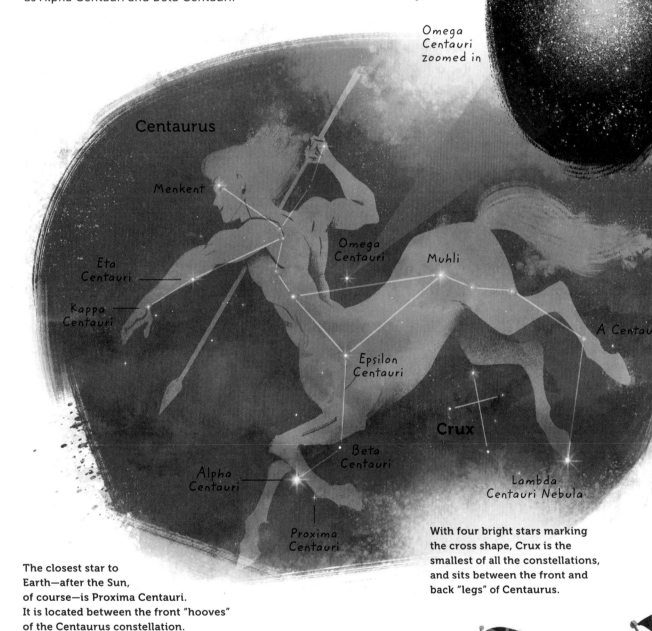

Omega Centauri zoomed in

Centaurus

Menkent

Eta Centauri

Kappa Centauri

Omega Centauri

Muhli

A Centauri

Epsilon Centauri

Crux

Lambda Centauri Nebula

Alpha Centauri

Beta Centauri

Proxima Centauri

The closest star to Earth—after the Sun, of course—is Proxima Centauri. It is located between the front "hooves" of the Centaurus constellation.

With four bright stars marking the cross shape, Crux is the smallest of all the constellations, and sits between the front and back "legs" of Centaurus.

Crux

The constellation called Crux (or Southern Cross) is easily visible from the southern hemisphere almost all year round. The Crux is famous in many countries and appears on national flags from Australia, New Zealand, Brazil, and Samoa.

CARINA CLOSE-UP

The great southern constellation of Carina (which means the keel, or bottom, of a ship) is made up of nine main stars, but has another 52 stars included in its vast shape. The fuzzy band of the Milky Way also runs through Carina.

Let's take a closer look at some of the highlights from this constellation.

Canopus

This is the brightest star on view in Carina, and the second-brightest in the night sky. Canopus shines more than 15,000 times more total light power than the Sun, but it lies more than 300 light-years away from Earth.

Miaplacidus

Miaplacidus is located about 110 light-years from Earth and is the second-brightest star in Carina. It is a giant star that has expanded to about 6.5 times the diameter of the Sun and has 3.5 times more mass than the Sun, too.

Carina Nebula

This is a 300-light-years-wide cloud of gas and dust that is a nursery for making new stars. The Carina Nebula is much larger than the Orion Nebula and more distant, at 7,500 light-years. It is the birthplace of some of the most extreme and massive stars known to humans.

Astronomers are using very powerful telescopes to study the earliest life phases of these amazing stars.

Canopus

Large magellanic cloud

Chi Carinae

Avior

CARINA

Aspidiske

Miaplacidus

Omega Carinae

Upsilon Carinae

Theta Carinae

Foramen

CARINA NEBULA

LAMBDA CENTAURI NEBULA

Carina Nebula zoomed in

Eta Carinae zoomed in

Eta Carinae

This is an incredibly powerful stellar system, containing at least two stars, about 7,500 light-years away from us. Compared to the Sun, Eta Carinae puts out 5 million times more light power and has at least 150 times more mass. Astronomers predict it will explode as a supernova within 3 million years.

SOUTHERN
CROSS

Delta Crucis

Epsilon Crucis

Acrux

Mimosa

Gacrux

17

LIFE CYCLES OF STARS

The stars you see in the night sky will not last forever. Every star has a life cycle, which from birth to death lasts millions, billions, or even trillions of years.

Stars shine because of the energy they make deep in their cores by nuclear fusion reactions. The main reaction is hydrogen being changed into helium, which makes an enormous amount of energy.

Stars begin to die when they complete all the fusion reactions that are possible and they run out of energy. The dying star collapses onto itself, pulled by gravity.

Stars like our Sun are lightweight stars. Our Sun is about 4.6 billion years old and has another 5 billion years of nuclear fusion fuel left. When that fuel runs out, its outer layers will bulge out to turn it into a red giant star.

How a star lives and dies depends mainly on how massive it was at birth in a nebula.

Eventually its outer layers will puff out to form a beautiful object known as a planetary nebula. Gravity will crush what's left of our Sun into a densely packed object about the size of Earth, called a white dwarf star. This dead star will slowly cool and then completely fade away.

Some stars are born with much more mass than our Sun. These are heavyweight stars. These mammoths live shorter lives and evolve over millions of years toward a violent and energetic end.

When these monsters run out of nuclear fusion fuel, they are destroyed in a powerful supernova explosion. The outer layers of the star get flung into space, and gravity crushes the leftover core. What remains can be a tightly packed neutron star that's just about 6 miles across. However, usually the leftovers are swallowed into the star's own gravity and end up as a stellar black hole.

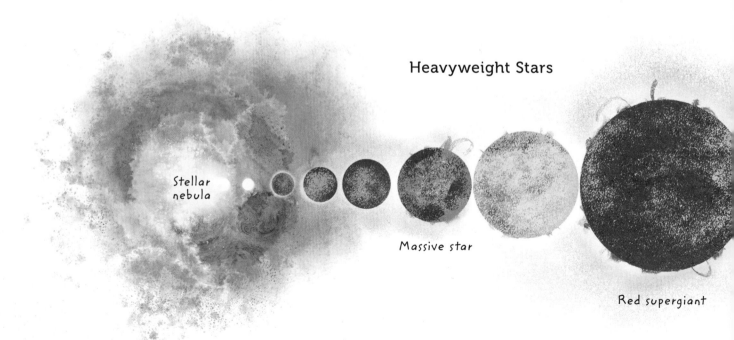

Heavyweight Stars

Stellar nebula

Massive star

Red supergiant

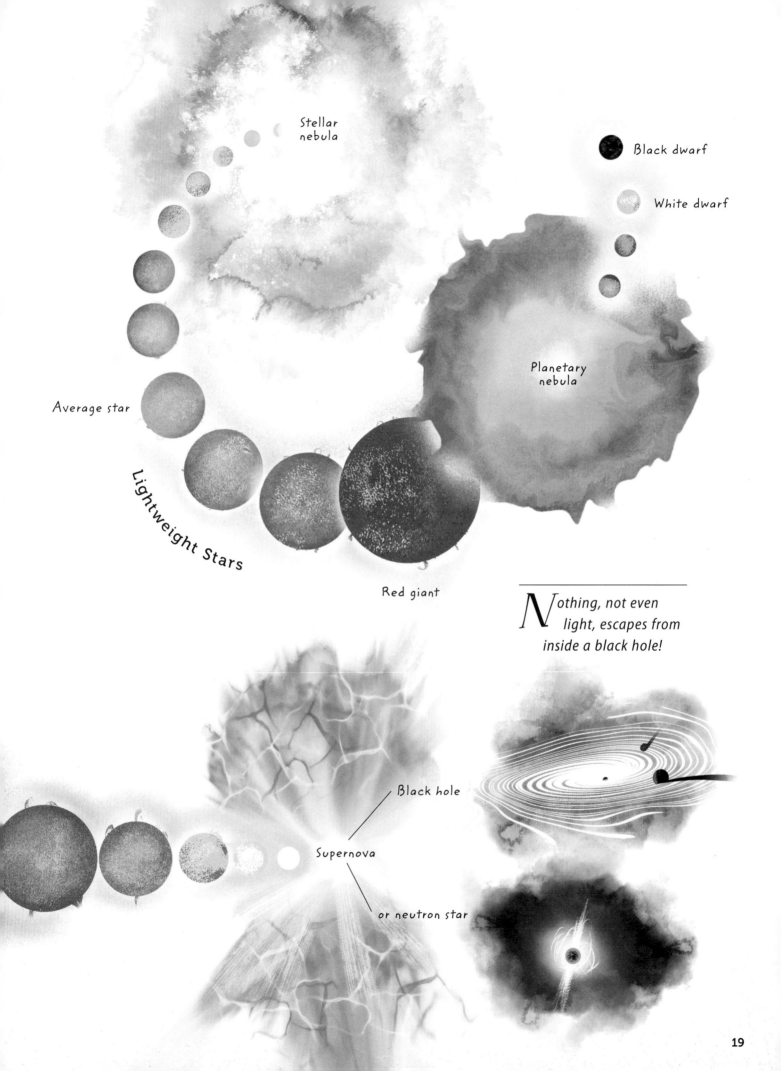

Stellar nebula

Black dwarf

White dwarf

Planetary nebula

Average star

Lightweight Stars

Red giant

Nothing, not even light, escapes from inside a black hole!

Black hole

Supernova

or neutron star

SPOTTING THE PLANETS

Planets are truly wonders of the night sky. At different times of the year, you can explore the five brightest planets—Mercury, Venus, Mars, Jupiter, and Saturn—wandering across the night sky.

Use the constellations and your mobile apps to guide you to parts of the sky where the planets can be spotted throughout the year.

Cancer

1st Feb

1st Dec

1st Jan

Leo

1st May

MARS'S MOVEMENTS

1st Jun

Explore Wandering

When you observe the sky night after night, the stars all appear in fixed positions when compared to each other. They seem painted against the inky black sky. The planets, however, move night after night against this fixed background of stars. From one month to the next, the position of a planet may even change from appearing inside one constellation to another.

KNOW WHY:

The planets wander when compared to the stars because of a projection effect. This happens because Earth and the other planets are moving in orbits, so the position of the planets as seen from Earth, and against a background of very distant stars, changes as the months pass.

Gemini

1st Nov

1st Mar

Explore Twinkling

Unlike the stars, the light from planets appears
to shine steadily and does not twinkle.

KNOW WHY:

All the planets are much closer to Earth than the stars—
Proxima Centauri is almost 180,000 times farther from
Earth than Mars! The stars' tiny pinpricks of far-away
light get jiggled easily by moving air in the Earth's
atmosphere, so the starlight seems to twinkle.

The closer light of the planets appears as a small disk
in the sky. The wider light beam coming from the
disk appears steadier in the sky.

PLANET HIGHLIGHTS

Here are some of the main features of the brightest five planets in the sky. Don't forget: binoculars or a small telescope can help reveal more details of a planet, such as its color, moons, or rings.

Jupiter

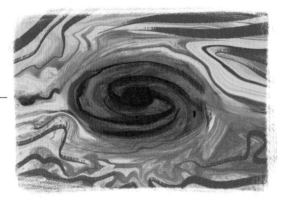

Look for two or three bands around the planet—the large cloud bands in Jupiter's very active atmosphere. A much larger telescope can show its Great Red Spot, a giant, spinning hurricane, visible for more than 300 years!

JUPITER, the king of planets, is fantastic to explore. Using a small telescope, you can spot many of its wonders.

Jupiter's moons in orbit

See if you can find the short line of tiny, star-like specks beside Jupiter. These are its four largest moons, known as Io, Europa, Ganymede, and Callisto. Watch these moons over several nights and you will see them change position as they orbit the giant planet.

Io

Europa

Ganymede

Callisto

Mercury

Surface of Mercury

To protect your eyes, only look for Mercury after sunset (in the west) or before sunrise (in the east). It looks like a dim star and is difficult to spot. Mercury is about 3,031 miles across its equator, compared with 7,926 miles for Earth.

MERCURY is the innermost planet in the solar system and never far away from the Sun in the sky.

Saturn

Large telescopes can reveal the biggest gaps between the rings and the details of the planet's largest moon, Titan.

Titan

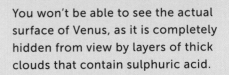

Saturn's rings

SATURN is an unforgettable wonder of the night sky, pale gold in color. Its magnificent rings can be seen with a small telescope.

Over many years, our view of the tilt of Saturn's rings changes, going from edge-on (barely visible) to a stunning face-on view. Saturn does appear considerably brighter when its wide rings are facing us. From edge-to-edge, the main ring system of Saturn would just about fit in the distance between the Earth and the Moon!

Venus

Like the Moon, Venus goes through phases such as crescent and quarter, depending on where it and Earth are in their orbits around the Sun. The phases are easy to see using a small telescope.

VENUS is the brightest planet in the night sky. At its most dazzling it has even been reported as a UFO!

You won't be able to see the actual surface of Venus, as it is completely hidden from view by layers of thick clouds that contain sulphuric acid.

Mars

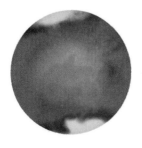

With a 7 centimeter-diameter telescope you can sometimes see the white, icy polar caps of Mars. Only a much larger telescope can reveal two tiny moons, Phobos and Deimos.

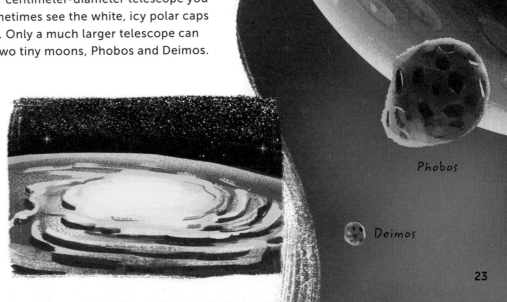

Phobos

Deimos

MARS is named after the Roman god of war because of its fierce, orange-red color. It has this fantastic color because its soil has rust particles in it.

SOLAR SYSTEM
TOUR

The solar system formed out of a giant cloud of spinning gas and dust about 4.6 billion years ago. It is made up of a star (the Sun), eight planets, at least five known dwarf planets, over 200 moons, and billions of small objects such as comets and asteroids.

In the outer solar system there are four huge gas planets: Jupiter, Saturn, Uranus, and Neptune. More than 1,300 Earths would fit inside Jupiter. The giant planets are mostly made of hydrogen and helium gases, and do not have any rocky surfaces.

NEPTUNE

URANUS

SATURN

JUPITER

All the giant gas planets have rings, though Saturn's are by far the largest and brightest. The rings around Jupiter, Uranus, and Neptune are dark and faint. Scientists had to use airborne observatories and spacecrafts to discover these much smaller ring systems.

Among the four rocky planets, Mars has two moons and Earth has one. The gas planets, however, have at least 200 moons among them. One of Jupiter's 79 known moons, Ganymede, is larger than the planet Mercury.

SUN

There are four rocky or
terrestrial planets, which in
order of distance from the Sun
are: Mercury, Venus, Earth, and
Mars. They have rocky surfaces
and rock and metallic interiors.

*E*arth is the only
*planet where life
is known to be thriving
today. Scientists estimate
that almost 9 million
different species of
plants and animals
live on our planet.*

MARS

VENUS

MERCURY

EARTH

ASTEROID BELT

There are billions of asteroids orbiting between Mars
and Jupiter, in a region known as the Asteroid Belt. It's
estimated that there are over 1 million asteroids bigger
than half a mile in size. If you could collect all
the material in the Asteroid Belt together,
it would make a world almost
as big as our Moon.

Astronomers have
discovered more than
4,000 planets orbiting other
stars. These are called exoplanets.
Some are gas, some are flowing with lava,
and some are much like Earth in size and temperature.
They may even have liquid water on their surfaces.

PHASES OF THE MOON

One of the most clearly seen changes in the night sky is the appearance of the Moon. Each month the Moon goes through a complete cycle of phases. Each phase relates to how much of the Moon's lit-up side we can see from Earth.

First Quarter

This phase happens about one week after the new moon. We are a quarter of the way through the cycle, and half of the Moon's lit-up face is visible from Earth.

Waxing Gibbous

At this phase, we see more than half of the sunlit side of the Moon.

Waxing Crescent

Waxing means gradually increasing. The Moon is being revealed as we see more of its lit-up side each night. A growing crescent shape appears.

New Moon

Let's start at the beginning of the cycle. The new moon is when the whole side of the Moon that faces Earth is dark, so the Moon is not really visible to us.

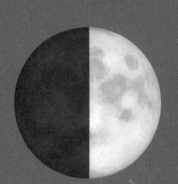

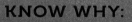

KNOW WHY:

Unlike the Sun, the Moon does not make and shine its own light. When we see the Moon, we are looking at sunlight reflected off its surface. So as the Moon orbits Earth, the Sun lights up different amounts of it. This makes it seem as though the Moon is changing shape, but it is just our view of it that is changing.

Full Moon

About two weeks after the new moon, the Moon is at its brightest and most brilliant. Its entire sunlit face is visible from Earth.

Waning Gibbous

Waning is an old English word that means decreasing. As the nights pass after the full moon, the sunlit part of the Moon starts to become less visible. At this phase, more than half of the daylight side of the Moon is visible.

Last Quarter

As with the first quarter, half of the Moon's lit-up side is visible once again. We are now three-quarters through the Moon's cycle of phases.

Waning Crescent

The Moon looks again like a thinning, slender crescent shape, as the visible sunlit part gets very small.

EARTH

Moon's Movements

Finally, about 29.5 days after the new moon, we are back to that same phase—an invisible Moon. A new cycle starts as the Moon continues its next orbit around Earth.

SURFACE OF THE MOON

The surface of the Moon is fantastic to explore using binoculars or a small telescope. There are some amazing features to look out for, such as craggy mountains, ancient lava plains, and deep craters.

Explore Maria

The dark patches you can see on the Moon are called maria (singular is mare), which means "seas" in the Latin language. These are not real seas of water, but in ancient times people thought they may be like our oceans.

KNOW WHY:

The maria on the Moon are flat plains of land that are covered in dark, ancient lava, which flooded there more than 3 billion years ago. The hot lava flowed into large basins on the Moon's surface, filled them up, and cooled down.

Use this map of the Moon to explore its surface.

Plato crater

MARE IMBRIUM

Archimedes crater

Aristarchus crater

Copernicus crater

Kepler crater

Ptolemaeus crater

OCEAN OF STORMS

MARE NUBIUM

Explore craters

Using this map, and binoculars or a telescope, try to find these impressive craters on the Moon. Tycho is the deepest, at just over 3 miles deep.

The best time to study the craters on the Moon is when it is less than half-lit. At waxing crescent or waning crescent, look along the line that divides the sunlit part from the dark part. This dividing line is called the terminator. Craters close to it show up beautifully in a telescope, with strong shadows being cast.

Posidonius crater

MARE SERENITATIS

Taurus Mountains

MARE CRISIUM

Menelaus crater

Plinius crater

Manilius crater

MARE TRANQUILLITATIS

Theophilus crater

Albategnius crater

MARE NECTARIS

Cyrillus crater

Catharina crater

Alphonsus crater

Arzachel crater

The largest mare on the Moon is almost twice as wide as the Earth's inner core!

Tycho crater

THE TERMINATOR

KNOW WHY:

Craters on the Moon form when small objects from space crash into its surface. The collisions happen with very high speeds and lots of energy, carving out the bowl shapes. Most of the impacts happened on the Moon about 3.8 billion years ago, when there were lot of rocks floating freely around in space, shortly after the planets formed.

MOON LANDING SITES

Have you ever imagined what it might be like to stand on the surface of the Moon? Astronauts traveled to the Moon on six different Apollo missions, between July 1969 and December 1972.

You too can explore the Moon by picking out the Apollo landing sites. You can try this when the phase of the Moon is full, or close to full. A 10 centimeters or larger telescope will allow you to look much closer, but you can still explore them just with your eyes.

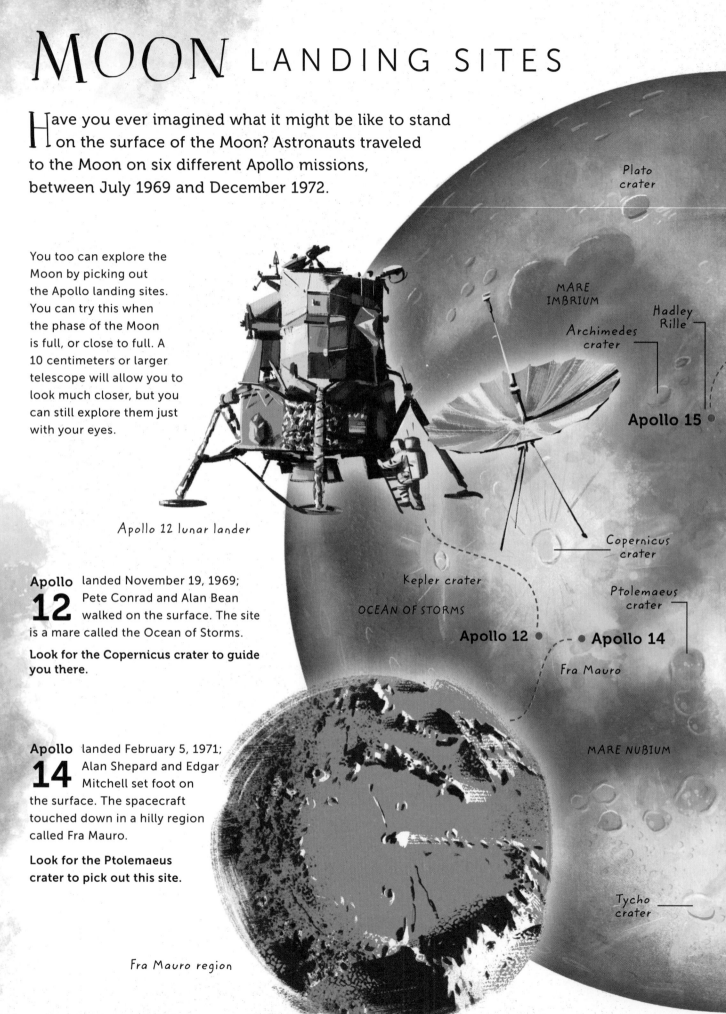

Apollo 12 lunar lander

Plato crater

MARE IMBRIUM

Archimedes crater

Hadley Rille

Apollo 15

Copernicus crater

Kepler crater

OCEAN OF STORMS

Ptolemaeus crater

Apollo 12 **Apollo 14**

Fra Mauro

MARE NUBIUM

Tycho crater

Apollo 12 landed November 19, 1969; Pete Conrad and Alan Bean walked on the surface. The site is a mare called the Ocean of Storms.

Look for the Copernicus crater to guide you there.

Apollo 14 landed February 5, 1971; Alan Shepard and Edgar Mitchell set foot on the surface. The spacecraft touched down in a hilly region called Fra Mauro.

Look for the Ptolemaeus crater to pick out this site.

Fra Mauro region

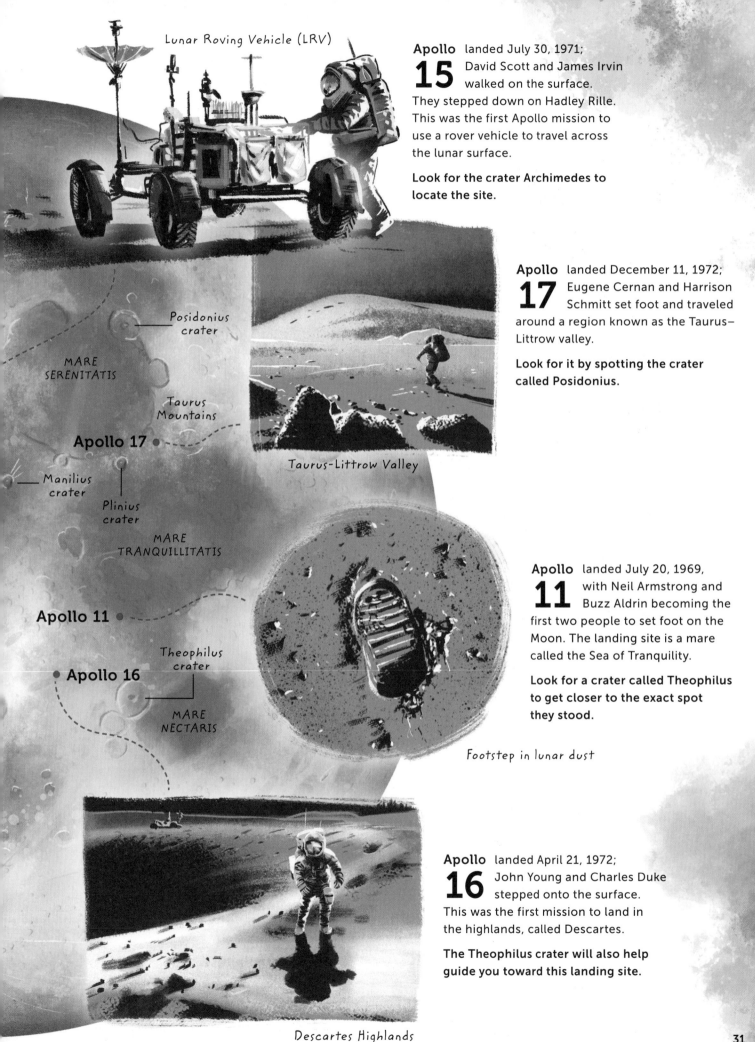

Lunar Roving Vehicle (LRV)

Apollo 15 landed July 30, 1971; David Scott and James Irvin walked on the surface. They stepped down on Hadley Rille. This was the first Apollo mission to use a rover vehicle to travel across the lunar surface.

Look for the crater Archimedes to locate the site.

Apollo 17 landed December 11, 1972; Eugene Cernan and Harrison Schmitt set foot and traveled around a region known as the Taurus–Littrow valley.

Look for it by spotting the crater called Posidonius.

Posidonius crater

MARE SERENITATIS

Taurus Mountains

Apollo 17

Taurus-Littrow Valley

Manilius crater

Plinius crater

MARE TRANQUILLITATIS

Apollo 11

Theophilus crater

Apollo 16

MARE NECTARIS

Apollo 11 landed July 20, 1969, with Neil Armstrong and Buzz Aldrin becoming the first two people to set foot on the Moon. The landing site is a mare called the Sea of Tranquility.

Look for a crater called Theophilus to get closer to the exact spot they stood.

Footstep in lunar dust

Apollo 16 landed April 21, 1972; John Young and Charles Duke stepped onto the surface. This was the first mission to land in the highlands, called Descartes.

The Theophilus crater will also help guide you toward this landing site.

Descartes Highlands

ECLIPSE OF THE MOON

Lunar eclipses are some of the easiest and most fascinating astronomical events to catch in the sky. All you need are clear skies and your eyes. Lunar eclipses occur on a full moon night, when the Sun, Earth, and Moon are arranged in a straight line. Depending on how much of the Moon falls into the shadow cast by the Earth, we get one of three types of lunar eclipse.

Daytime

Earth

Nighttime

Earth's orbit

Partial lunar eclipse

A fraction, but not all, of the Moon passes into the darkest part of the Earth's shadow—the Umbra. Partial eclipses are easy to observe, with part of the full moon clearly going dark.

PARTIAL ECLIPSE

What we see from Earth

UMBRA

PENUMBRA

The weaker shadow cast by Earth is called the penumbra. The darker shadow is the umbra.

BLOOD MOON

Moon's orbit

PENUMBRAL ECLIPSE

Penumbral lunar eclipse

This is when the Moon is only faintly in the Earth's weaker shadow. This eclipse is hardest to observe with the naked eye.

Total lunar eclipse

In this case the entire Moon passes into the Earth's darkest shadow. The period of totality—when the Moon is completely in the Earth's shadow—can last up to 2 hours. These eclipses happen roughly twice every 3 years. A total lunar eclipse is known as a Blood Moon, as it sometimes takes on beautiful shades of red, brown, and orange.

KNOW WHY:

Colorful eclipses happen because of the way way sunlight passes through the Earth's atmosphere. As sunlight strikes our atmosphere, shorter wavelengths of light, such as blue, are scattered outwards. Longer wavelengths, such as red, are bent into the Earth's shadowy area. When this light hits the Moon's surface during a total lunar eclipse, we see the blood-red reflection, similar to how skies appear red during sunrise and sunset.

ORIGINS AND FEATURES OF THE MOON

The Moon formed about the same time as the Earth, roughly 4.5 billion years ago. Astronomers believe that a rocky body about the size of Mars crashed into Earth, and the impact threw up a lot of material.

This debris went into orbit around the Earth and was slowly gathered together by the force of gravity to form the Moon.

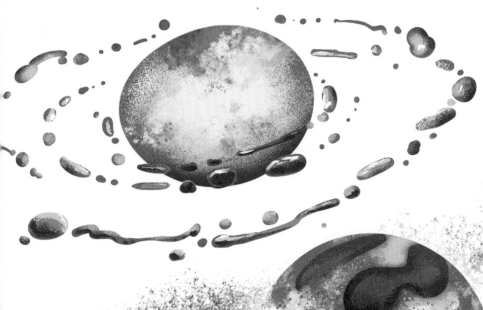

Between 3 and 4 billion years ago, the Moon was struck by lots of space rocks, which crashed into its surface, releasing molten rock from beneath. This lava flowed into its basins and craters, forming plains.

During the first 600 million years of the Moon's life, a vast number of asteroids and comets crashed into its surface, forming craters. Today we can still see many of them because the Moon does not have a strong atmosphere. Without wind and rain, the craters have not eroded away as they have on Earth over billions of years.

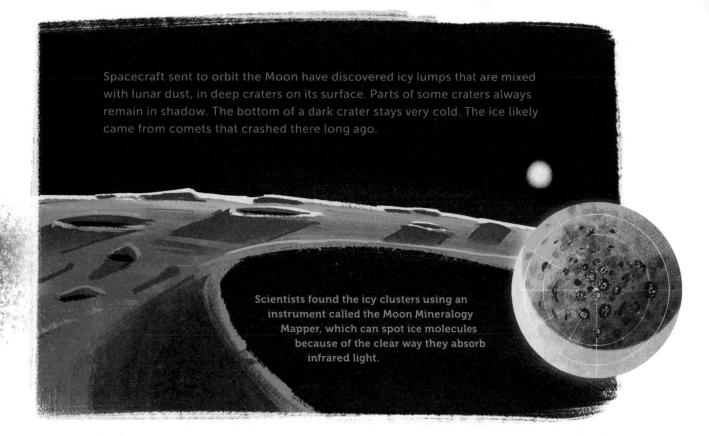

Spacecraft sent to orbit the Moon have discovered icy lumps that are mixed with lunar dust, in deep craters on its surface. Parts of some craters always remain in shadow. The bottom of a dark crater stays very cold. The ice likely came from comets that crashed there long ago.

Scientists found the icy clusters using an instrument called the Moon Mineralogy Mapper, which can spot ice molecules because of the clear way they absorb infrared light.

Meteor Showers

AT certain times of the year nature puts on its own fireworks shows. These exciting displays are called meteor showers and you don't need any special equipment to enjoy them!

With adult supervision, avoid as much light pollution as possible and go to a dark place. Get comfortable—lie down on your back or in a reclining chair, and gaze up at the clear night sky. You will need to be patient and ready to spend a few hours outside.

Swift-Tuttle debris field

Here are three great meteor showers to enjoy from both hemispheres on Earth.

Explore Perseids

A bright display visible from both hemispheres is the Perseids shower. It appears to emerge from the constellation of Perseus between around July 17 to August 24 each year. At its peak (usually around August 12–13), up to 80 meteors per hour may be on show. You might even be treated to a few fireballs, which are extremely bright meteors with long tails.

Perseus

Look toward Perseus from July to August to see the Perseids.

SUN

Earth's position in August

Earth's orbit around the Sun

Swift-Tuttle in orbit around the Sun

EARTH

KNOW WHY:

The Perseids are caused when the Earth passes through debris left behind by a comet called Swift-Tuttle. This comet last passed near Earth during its orbit around the Sun in 1992, and the next time will be in 2126.

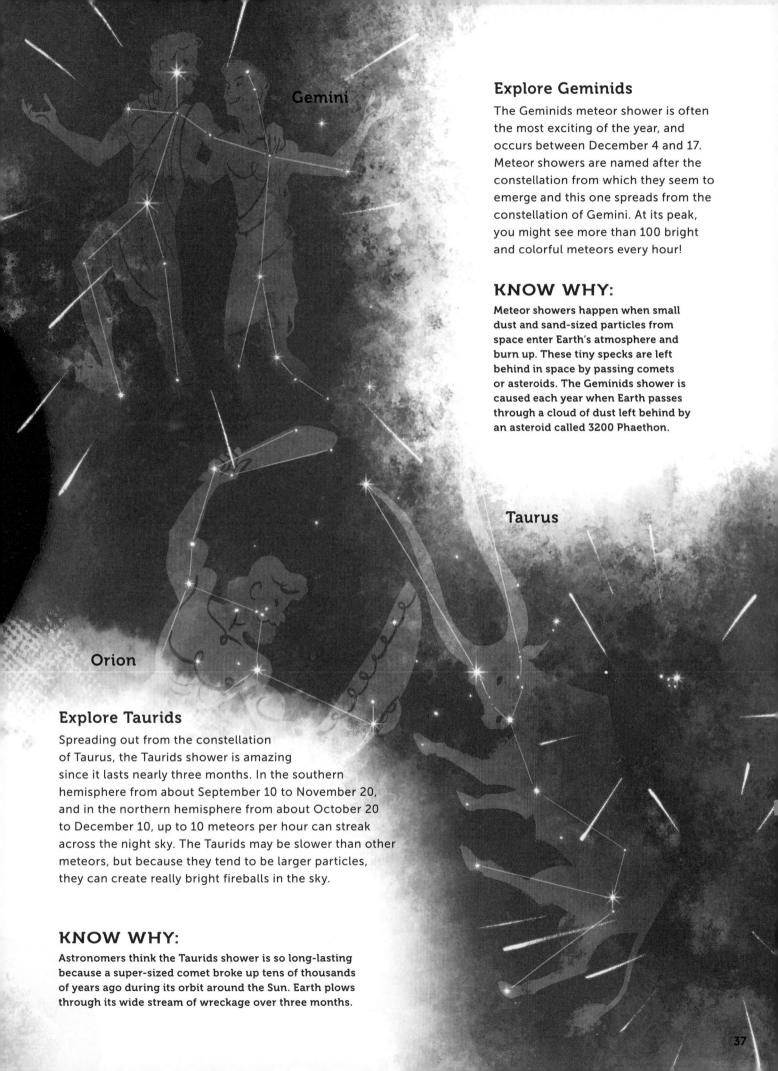

Gemini

Explore Geminids

The Geminids meteor shower is often the most exciting of the year, and occurs between December 4 and 17. Meteor showers are named after the constellation from which they seem to emerge and this one spreads from the constellation of Gemini. At its peak, you might see more than 100 bright and colorful meteors every hour!

KNOW WHY:

Meteor showers happen when small dust and sand-sized particles from space enter Earth's atmosphere and burn up. These tiny specks are left behind in space by passing comets or asteroids. The Geminids shower is caused each year when Earth passes through a cloud of dust left behind by an asteroid called 3200 Phaethon.

Taurus

Orion

Explore Taurids

Spreading out from the constellation of Taurus, the Taurids shower is amazing since it lasts nearly three months. In the southern hemisphere from about September 10 to November 20, and in the northern hemisphere from about October 20 to December 10, up to 10 meteors per hour can streak across the night sky. The Taurids may be slower than other meteors, but because they tend to be larger particles, they can create really bright fireballs in the sky.

KNOW WHY:

Astronomers think the Taurids shower is so long-lasting because a super-sized comet broke up tens of thousands of years ago during its orbit around the Sun. Earth plows through its wide stream of wreckage over three months.

ASTEROIDS

Objects floating around the solar system sometimes get very close to Earth. There is always a risk one might strike our planet. Though this is very unlikely, there are astronomers around the world keeping track of them. One example of bodies they watch out for are asteroids.

Asteroids are leftovers from the matter that formed the Sun, planets, and moons of the solar system, billions of years ago. They are small, mostly rocky bodies that orbit the Sun. Most are in a region between the orbits of Mars and Jupiter known as the Asteroid Belt. There are almost 2 million asteroids longer than half a mile in this Belt, and many billions of smaller ones.

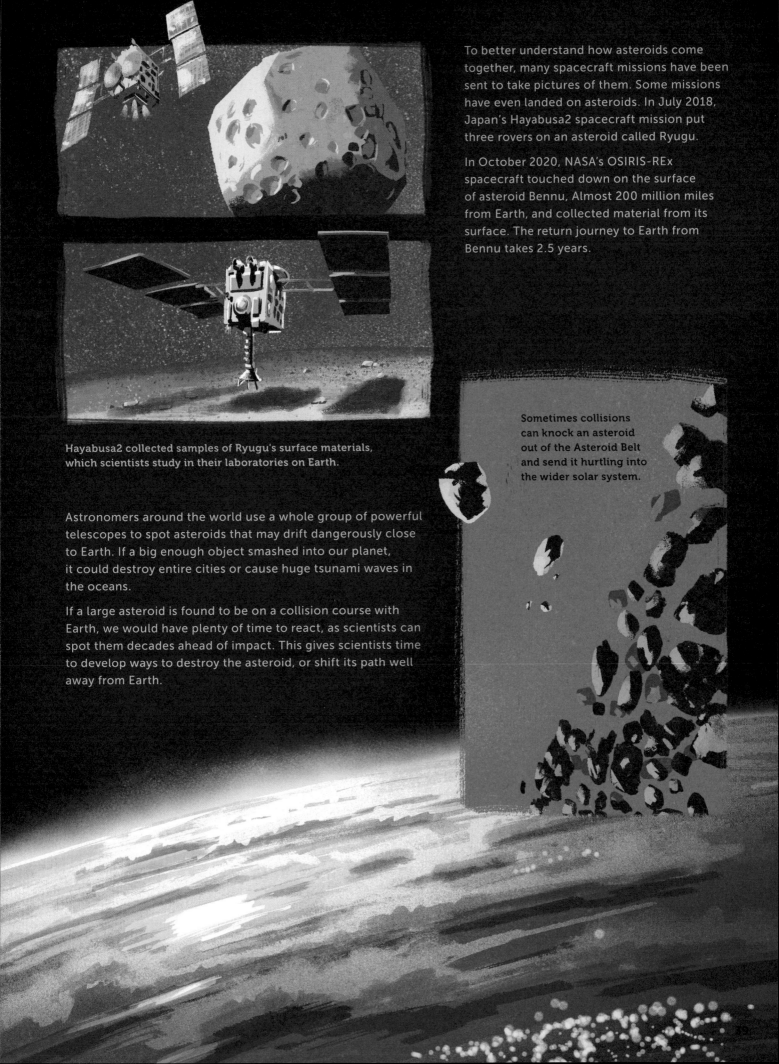

To better understand how asteroids come together, many spacecraft missions have been sent to take pictures of them. Some missions have even landed on asteroids. In July 2018, Japan's Hayabusa2 spacecraft mission put three rovers on an asteroid called Ryugu.

In October 2020, NASA's OSIRIS-REx spacecraft touched down on the surface of asteroid Bennu, Almost 200 million miles from Earth, and collected material from its surface. The return journey to Earth from Bennu takes 2.5 years.

Hayabusa2 collected samples of Ryugu's surface materials, which scientists study in their laboratories on Earth.

Astronomers around the world use a whole group of powerful telescopes to spot asteroids that may drift dangerously close to Earth. If a big enough object smashed into our planet, it could destroy entire cities or cause huge tsunami waves in the oceans.

If a large asteroid is found to be on a collision course with Earth, we would have plenty of time to react, as scientists can spot them decades ahead of impact. This gives scientists time to develop ways to destroy the asteroid, or shift its path well away from Earth.

Sometimes collisions can knock an asteroid out of the Asteroid Belt and send it hurtling into the wider solar system.

COMETS

Bright comets are stunning objects in the night sky. A truly great comet—with a spectacular, flowing tail stretched across most of the sky—is a rare but unforgettable sight.

Comets are small, rocky bodies, just a few miles across. They are made of rock, dust, and ice; you can imagine them as giant, dirty snowballs! They orbit the Sun in long, oval-shaped paths, but only form a tail when gliding nearer to the Sun.

ION TAIL

Made of electrons and gas atoms pulled out of the coma by ultraviolet light from the Sun

DUST TAIL

Made of tiny particles, usually seen as fluffy and curved

Astronomers study comets because they can teach us a great deal about the original matter that came together to build the planets and moons. Comets, along with asteroids, may also have delivered most of the water we have on Earth.

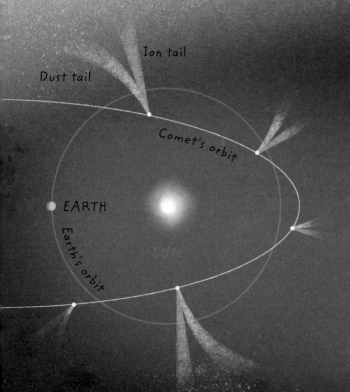

Ion tail

Dust tail

Comet's orbit

EARTH

Earth's orbit

SUN

KNOW WHY:

As a comet gets close to the Sun, the star's energy warms the ice on the comet, causing it to boil off. The heated comet starts to spew out gas and dust, which then forms its tail.

Meanwhile, there is a steady stream of particles flowing from the Sun, known as the solar wind. This stream pushes on the comet, which is why the tail of a comet always points away from the Sun.

Astronomers cannot be sure when the next great comet will grace the night sky. Over the past 50 years, a bright comet has appeared about once every 5–10 years. When a comet does appear, it won't just streak across the sky in a flash, like a meteor. Since comets are usually millions of miles away, they stay in the sky night after night for several weeks.

Ice and rock

COMA

A cloud of gases, mostly hydrogen, around the nucleus; can be over 600,000 miles across

NUCLEUS

Solid core of a comet, usually only half a mile to six miles in diameter

Direction of comet's orbit

NUCLEUS

Direction of sunlight hitting the coma

Comet *NEOWISE*

During July 2020, observers were treated to the first bright comet that could be seen with the unaided eye in the northern hemisphere this century. It was named Comet NEOWISE, after NASA's Near-Earth Object Wide-field Infrared Survey Explorer (NEOWISE) satellite mission, which first discovered the comet.

The comet zipped through the inner solar system, forming a beautiful tail. Comet NEOWISE was special as it has a very long orbit around the Sun. The last generation of humans to see it before us would have lived during the third millennium BCE!

COMET ORIGINS

There are two huge areas in the solar system from which comets emerge, the Kuiper Belt and the Oort Cloud. The inner solar system includes the Sun and planets Mercury, Venus, Earth, and Mars, out to the Asteroid Belt between Mars and Jupiter. Beyond the asteroid belt is the outer solar system. This is the realm of the giant gas planets and the donut-shaped Kuiper Belt. All this is set in the middle of the enormous Oort Cloud.

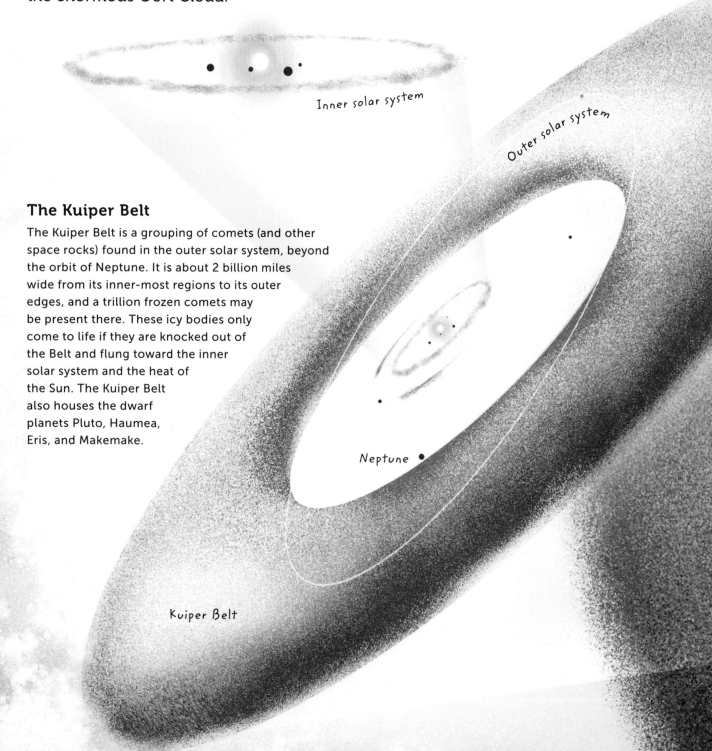

Inner solar system

Outer solar system

The Kuiper Belt

The Kuiper Belt is a grouping of comets (and other space rocks) found in the outer solar system, beyond the orbit of Neptune. It is about 2 billion miles wide from its inner-most regions to its outer edges, and a trillion frozen comets may be present there. These icy bodies only come to life if they are knocked out of the Belt and flung toward the inner solar system and the heat of the Sun. The Kuiper Belt also houses the dwarf planets Pluto, Haumea, Eris, and Makemake.

Neptune ●

Kuiper Belt

Oort Cloud

Oort Cloud

The Oort Cloud is a vast, ball-shaped region of icy objects that surrounds the Sun, all the planets, and the Kuiper Belt. The Oort Cloud stretches as far as 8.7 trillion miles from the Sun (still only about a quarter of the distance to Proxima Centauri); however, it could be even bigger than we estimate!

Trillions of comets are believed to originate from the Oort Cloud, each taking more than 200 years to complete one lap around the Sun.

The auroras are one of nature's most spectacular light shows.

NORTHERN AND SOUTHERN LIGHTS

These bands of blue, green, and red streaking across the night sky are called Northern Lights (or aurora borealis) in the northern hemisphere. In the southern hemisphere they are known as Southern Lights (or aurora australis). Displays of auroras in the night sky tell us something electric is happening in the atmosphere.

Auroras are best seen from regions that are closer to the poles of Earth, such as Iceland, Norway, northern Canada, Alaska, Tasmania, and New Zealand. There are apps for mobile devices that give alerts when an aurora is likely to happen.

You don't need any special equipment to see an aurora, just patience and enthusiasm! Pick a dark night, away from the glare of city lights, and wear warm clothing. Let your eyes get adjusted to the dark and look toward the horizon.

Auroras will ripple and sway, almost like curtains blowing gently in the night sky. The lights can disappear suddenly and then re-form. Note how they change in color and shape. Use a camera to take lots of pictures. With luck you might capture an astronomical masterpiece!

KNOW WHY:

The light from an aurora occurs when electrified particles, mostly from the Sun, travel across space. The particles strike into the Earth's magnetic field, where they get trapped and dragged into the planet's atmosphere. This results in glowing halos of dancing light, similar to how neon tube lights glow on shop signs.

Earth isn't the only place with auroras. Saturn's auroras vividly light up both its poles. Saturn's auroras can't be seen with the naked eye, though, as they shine in ultraviolet light.

THE SUN-EARTH CONNECTION

Auroras are a stunning reminder of how the Sun and Earth are connected. Streams of these electrically charged particles (mostly electrons and protons) continually flow out of the Sun in all directions. When they arrive at Earth, we get to see them react colorfully with molecules as they are guided across our sky, toward the two poles.

Solar flare

CME

At times, the Sun can become very active and throw out enormous amounts of matter and energy. Some of these sudden bursts are called flares. The largest flares blast tons of super-hot gas into space. The amount of energy released in a single solar flare can be millions of times greater than the energy of a volcano erupting on Earth!

At its most active, the Sun can also spew giant bubbles of hot gas, known as coronal mass ejections (or CMEs). These are awesome clouds of electrified gas that can swell to 6.2 million miles and move through space at speeds of 6.2 million miles per hour. Just two to three days after their release from the Sun's surface, CMEs can strike Earth, causing huge electrical storms above us.

The energetic particles pushed out by the Sun during flares and CMEs can have severe effects on Earth. Scientists use telescopes in space to track solar eruptions. You can think of it as keeping an eye on the space weather.

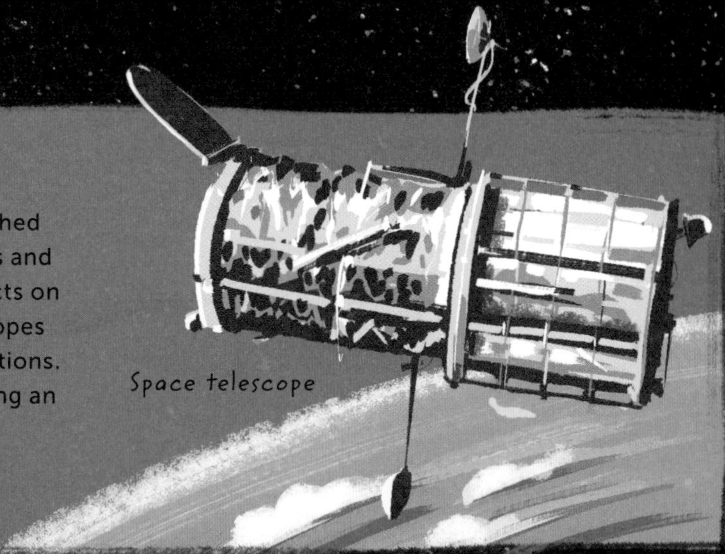

Space telescope

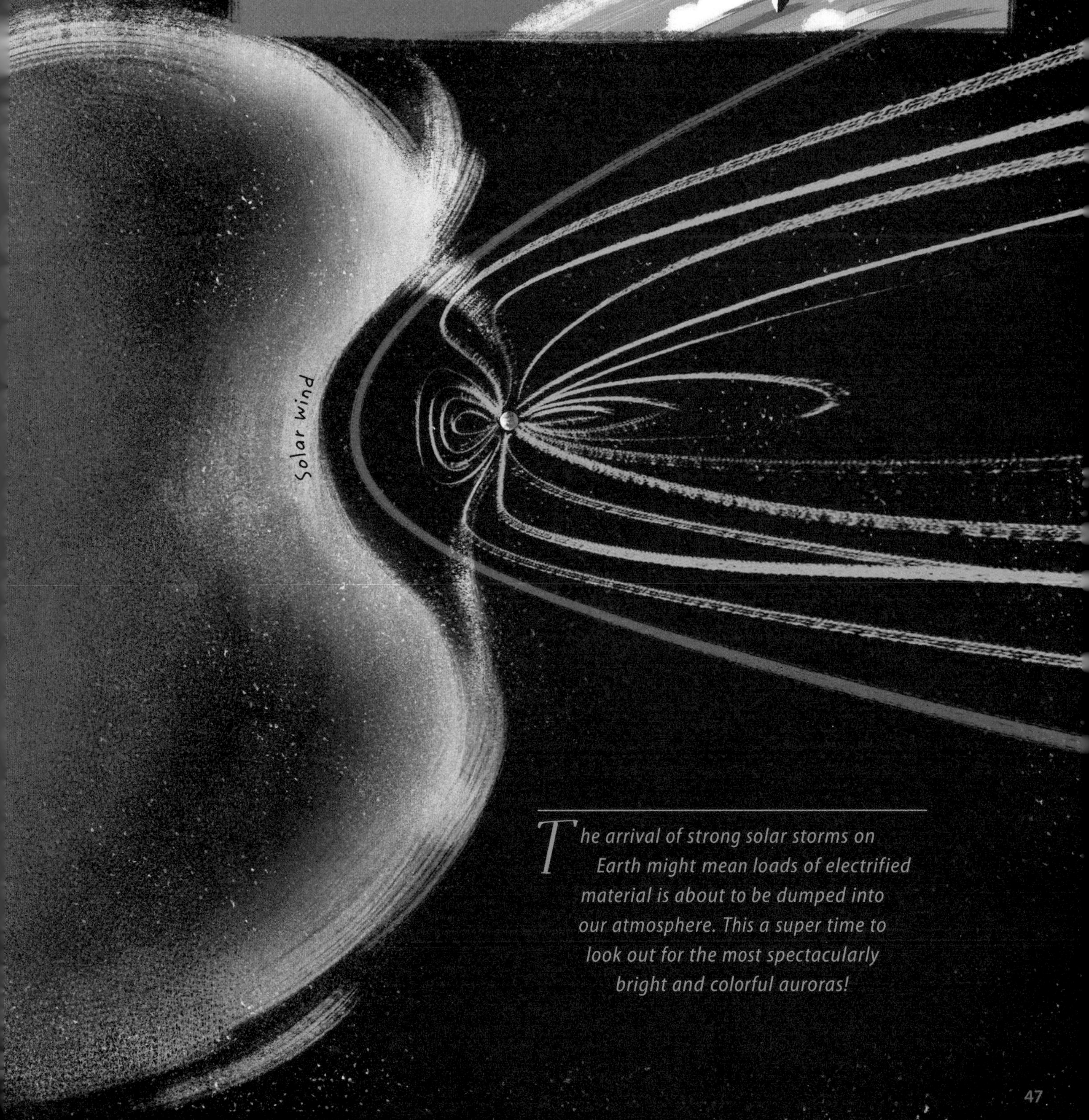

Solar wind

The arrival of strong solar storms on Earth might mean loads of electrified material is about to be dumped into our atmosphere. This a super time to look out for the most spectacularly bright and colorful auroras!

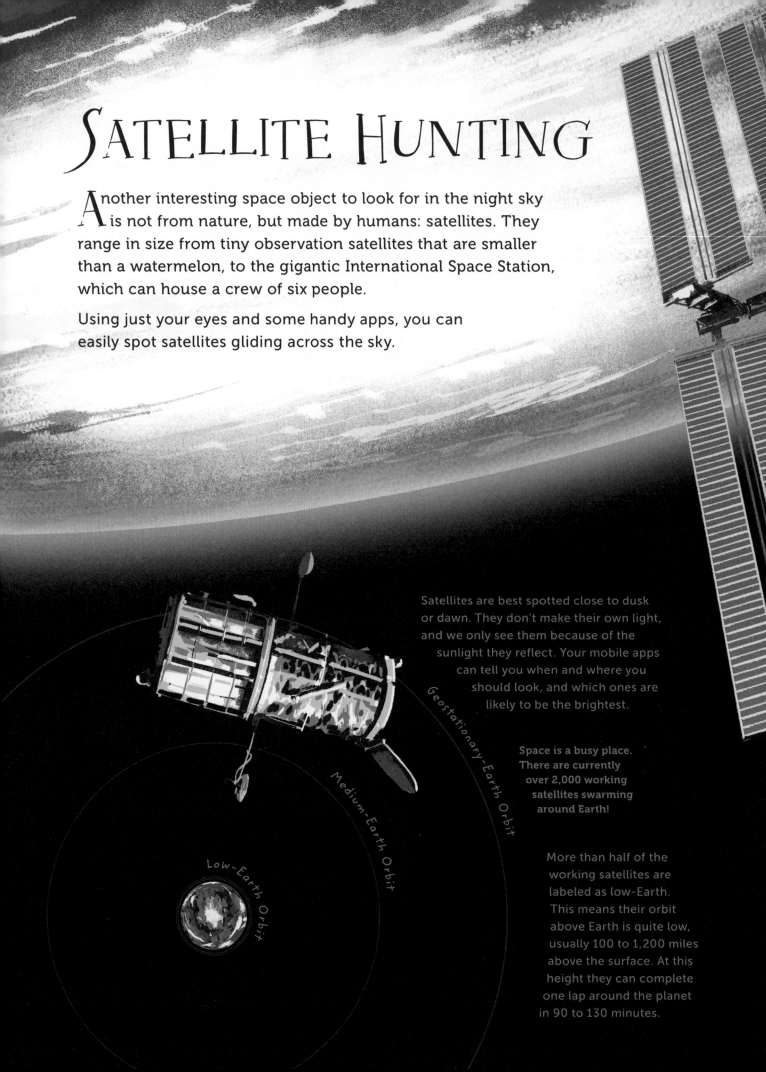

SATELLITE HUNTING

Another interesting space object to look for in the night sky is not from nature, but made by humans: satellites. They range in size from tiny observation satellites that are smaller than a watermelon, to the gigantic International Space Station, which can house a crew of six people.

Using just your eyes and some handy apps, you can easily spot satellites gliding across the sky.

Satellites are best spotted close to dusk or dawn. They don't make their own light, and we only see them because of the sunlight they reflect. Your mobile apps can tell you when and where you should look, and which ones are likely to be the brightest.

Space is a busy place. There are currently over 2,000 working satellites swarming around Earth!

More than half of the working satellites are labeled as low-Earth. This means their orbit above Earth is quite low, usually 100 to 1,200 miles above the surface. At this height they can complete one lap around the planet in 90 to 130 minutes.

Geostationary-Earth Orbit

Medium-Earth Orbit

Low-Earth Orbit

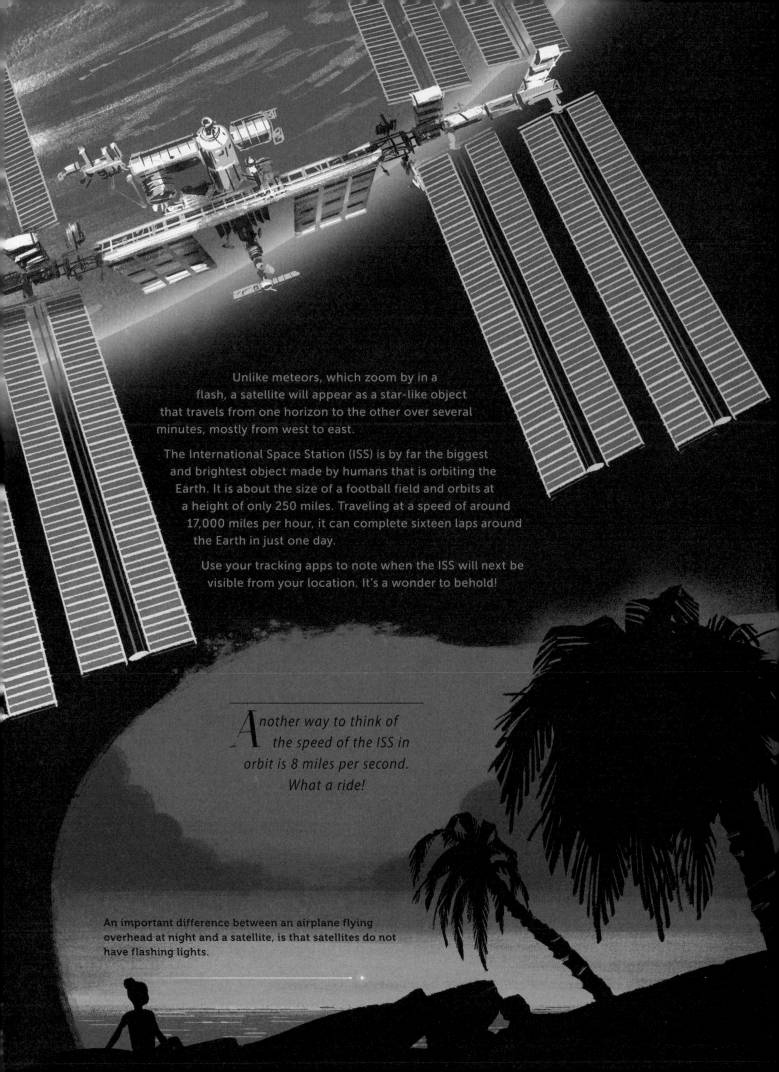

Unlike meteors, which zoom by in a
flash, a satellite will appear as a star-like object
that travels from one horizon to the other over several
minutes, mostly from west to east.

The International Space Station (ISS) is by far the biggest
and brightest object made by humans that is orbiting the
Earth. It is about the size of a football field and orbits at
a height of only 250 miles. Traveling at a speed of around
17,000 miles per hour, it can complete sixteen laps around
the Earth in just one day.

Use your tracking apps to note when the ISS will next be
visible from your location. It's a wonder to behold!

*Another way to think of
the speed of the ISS in
orbit is 8 miles per second.
What a ride!*

An important difference between an airplane flying
overhead at night and a satellite, is that satellites do not
have flashing lights.

SPACE JUNK

Sadly, our waste is not only piling up on Earth, it is also building up in orbit around our planet. Known as "space junk", this debris has been growing ever since the Space Age started, with the launch of the Sputnik 1 satellite, in 1957. Since then, there have been about 5,000 more spacecraft and satellite launches around the world. Unfortunately, success in space exploration has also led to lots of human-made materials ending up as junk in space.

Rocket parts

Lost tools

Paint chips

Space junk includes old, inactive satellites, stages of rockets, and much smaller parts such as nuts, bolts, tools, and chips of paint. Scientists use telescopes and radar to track the junk. They estimate that about 23,000 bits of rubbish larger than 4 inches in size are orbiting up there. Even the tiniest bits can cause massive damage if they smash into working satellites, because they are moving at speeds faster than a bullet! They are also a risk to astronauts working in and around the International Space Station.

Humans are likely to launch more and more satellites every year, as we need them for communication (cell phones, for example), weather forecasting, and scientific study. So we need to clean up space for them.

Creative clean-up

Scientists have started to invent ways to remove or reduce space junk. One idea is to use an electric space whip, which could knock debris out of its orbit and plunge it down to burn up in Earth's atmosphere. Another idea is to use spacecraft that launch giant nets to capture large bits of junk. Perhaps one day we might even work out ways of bringing the rubbish back to Earth to recycle it!

Old satellites

Space-cleaning machines could have several different designs, including roping in rubbish with a net, refuelling satellites to extend their lives, or using robotic arms to grab old satellites and drag them to safer spots.

THE MILKY WAY

A beautiful wonder of space is the sight of the Milky Way stretching all the way across the night sky. We actually live inside the spiral-shaped galaxy known as the Milky Way Galaxy. It is mostly a flat, plate-like shape, with our Sun and solar system located about two-thirds away from the center.

The band of the Milky Way is quite faint, so you will need to observe it from a location well away from the glare of city lights. You will also need to pick a clear, cloudless night, and it'll help if the Moon's phase is new moon, so that the night is really dark. Give your eyes about 20 minutes to be at their best for spotting faint objects.

Sagittarius

The southern hemisphere offers the most chances to see the Milky Way and its bright center, which lies toward the constellation of Sagittarius. In the southern hemisphere, you can see the Milky Way band high in the sky in the hours before sunrise between April and May, near midnight from June to August, and soon after sunset between mid-August and September.

In the northern hemisphere, you will get the best views between August and September. The views in the northern hemisphere are not as clear since the summer nights are only truly dark for a few hours. The farther north you are, the band of the Milky Way will be low toward the horizon when looking south.

OUR HOME GALAXY

The Sun and all the stars we see at night belong to our Milky Way Galaxy. It is a sprawling, spiral-shaped galaxy made of 200–400 billion stars, plus lots of gas and dust. The whole Milky Way is held together by the force of gravity.

We are here

The Milky Way has spiral arms that emerge from its center. Our solar system is on one of these arms, about 26,000 light-years from the Milky Way's center. From this spot the Sun (and solar system) moves around the center of our galaxy at a speed of 516,000 miles per hour, and takes 230 million years to complete just one orbit.

Side view

Imagine the Sun is the size of a grain of sand. Earth would then be an even tinier speck about a third of an inch from the grain. On this scale, the entire Milky Way Galaxy would include at least 200 billion of these grains of sand, stretching roughly 50,000 miles!

Bulge

The central part of the Milky Way is a rounded, bulge shape. Imagine it looking like two fried eggs stuck back-to-back: the yellow yolks make up the bulge, and the egg whites are the flat disk where the spiral arms are found.

SUN

BULGE

HALO

Halo

Our galaxy is surrounded by an enormous, ball-shaped region known as the halo. The halo contains over 150 tightly packed groups, called globular clusters, each of which can contain millions of very old stars. Astronomers have also discovered large amounts of a strange type of matter known as dark matter in the halo.

SUPER-MASSIVE
BLACK HOLE

Central Beast

Astronomers have discovered that there is a super-massive black hole at the very center of our galaxy. Lying toward the constellation of Sagittarius, the black hole has a mass of about 4 million of our Suns.

*When searching for
other galaxies,
familiar constellations
can point you to the right
patch of sky from which
to start your hunt.*

Canopus

DORADO

The LMC

The Large Magellanic
Cloud is between the
constellations Dorado and
Mensa. It appears as a faint
smudge and can be spotted
all night, every night of the
year, from nearly all parts of the
southern hemisphere, as long as
the skies are clear.

Large
Magellanic
Cloud

Achernar

CARINA

HYDRUS

VOLANS

MENSA

Small
Magellanic
Cloud

The SMC

The Small Magellanic Cloud is south of the Large Magellanic Cloud.
It is fainter and smaller. Look for the bright star called Achernar in
the constellation Eridanus. If you hold your fists on top of each other
at arm's length, and drop this distance in the sky below Achernar,
you will be close to where the Small Magellanic Cloud sits.

ANDROMEDA AND THE
MAGELLANIC CLOUDS

There are billions of galaxies beyond our Milky Way Galaxy. But the
Universe is so enormous that most of these galaxies are many millions
of light years away from us. They are extremely faint, and can only be seen
through large and powerful telescopes.

The Andromeda Galaxy

Andromeda is a beautiful, spiral-shaped galaxy about 2.5 million light-years away. This means that light takes 2.5 million years to reach us from Andromeda, so we see it today as it looked 2.5 million years ago!

From the northern hemisphere, start by picking out Cassiopeia's *W* shape. Use the bottom-right point as an arrowhead and you will get close to Andromeda: a faint, puffy patch in the sky. With binoculars or a telescope, you can make out Andromeda's brighter core and oval shape.

Cassiopeia

Andromeda

There are, however, three nearby galaxies that are just about visible with the naked eye. Once again, you'll need a dark location on a clear, Moon-less night.

If you live in or visit the southern hemisphere, you can look out for two galaxies that are close neighbors, the Large and Small Magellanic Clouds (LMC and SMC). In the northern hemisphere, the Andromeda Galaxy swirls in the sky near Cassiopeia.

MAIN GALAXY TYPES

Astronomers estimate there may be up to 2 trillion galaxies in the Universe. Each one is a vast collection of stars, planets, gas, and dust held together by the force of gravity. The galaxies do not all have the same shape or size. Galaxies with less than 1 billion stars are thought to be small, while the grandest galaxies can house trillions of stars!

Galaxies are grouped into three main types, called spiral, elliptical, and irregular.

SPIRAL GALAXY

Our Milky Way Galaxy is a spiral galaxy. Spiral galaxies are stunning, pinwheel shapes. They are made up of a thin, flat disk and a large bulge at the center. The disk contains the spiral arms, which are packed with bright stars, planets, gas, and dust. The disk is surrounded by an enormous halo, which not only contains the oldest stars, but also a mysterious type of matter called dark matter.

IRREGULAR GALAXY

As suggested by the name, these galaxies do not have any regular shape. Irregular galaxies have lots of gas and dust, out of which new stars continue to be made. The Large and Small Magellanic Clouds are two irregular galaxies, and the galaxy shown here is a starburst galaxy called M82.

ELLIPTICAL GALAXY

Elliptical galaxies contain mostly old stars, and have very little leftover gas and dust. These galaxies are shaped like fuzzy footballs. The largest-known galaxies in the Universe are ellipticals, some of which can be 6 million light-years across.

Some super-powerful galaxies, called quasars, can shine up to 100,000 times brighter than the Milky Way Galaxy!

ACTIVITIES
SUN, EARTH, AND MOON ORRERY

In this activity you can build a simple cardboard model that shows how the Earth orbits the Sun, and the Moon goes around the Earth. You can use this orrery to understand the positions of the three bodies creating the different phases of the Moon, and how lunar and solar eclipses occur.

YOU WILL NEED:

white cardboard
scissors
3 metal paper connectors
compass to draw circles
paints

1. Draw three circles on the card using the compass. You will need a 7-inch-diameter circle for the Sun, 3.5 inches for the Earth, and 1 inch for the Moon. (Note that these are not accurate relative sizes since the Sun is really 109 times wider than the Earth!)

2. Cut out the three circles and paint them: yellow for the Sun, blue oceans and green continents for the Earth, and gray for the Moon.

3. Cut out two strips of card, each about a little over half an inch wide. One strip should be about 8.5 inches long and the other about 3.5 inches long.

4. Connect the end of the long strip to the center of the Sun, using one metal connector. Close the connector around the back of the Sun.

5. Connect the end of the shorter strip to the center of the back of the Moon, using the second connector. Close the connector around the back of the Moon.

6. Connect the other end of the short strip to the center of the Earth using the last connector. Don't close it just yet.

7. Connect the remaining end of the long strip to the center of the back of the Earth, using the same pin from Step 6. Close the connector onto both strips.

MOON
The diameter of the Moon should be about 1 inch

SUN
The diameter of the Sun should be 7 inches

metal paper connector

EARTH
The diameter of the Earth should be 3.5 inches

Moon to Earth arm is 3.5 inches

Sun to Earth arm is 8.5 inches

SOLAR ECLIPSE

LUNAR ECLIPSE

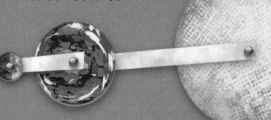

ON THE MOON

Moon surfaces and many rocky planets are scarred by craters that vary in size from a few feet to hundreds of miles in diameter. Here's a fascinating activity for you to explore how different craters are made and how surface soil is dug up.

YOU WILL NEED:

white flour
hot chocolate powder
marbles (varied sizes)
a large, shallow metal pan

1. Fill the pan to a little over half an inch deep with the white flour. Lightly sprinkle the powdered chocolate to cover the surface of the flour. The chocolate and white flour act as the upper soil and deeper layers of the Moon.

2. To make a model of the Moon's surface, now drop marbles one at a time onto the pan. Drop the marbles straight down rather than throwing them in. The marbles act as the crashing asteroids and comets.

3. Notice how craters are made in the pan by the marbles. The soil (white flour) is dug up and brought to the surface. The biggest, deepest craters on the Moon, too, reveal deeper layers in the Moon's crust.

4. Drop different sized marbles to see the different impact sizes.

5. Also drop the same size marbles from different heights. Marbles dropped from the greatest height will have a greater speed when they reach the surface of the pan.

These marbles will make larger craters because they have more energy.

6. Try dropping marbles at an angle rather than straight down and see how the shape of the dents—and spread of flour—changes.

You won't believe how realistic your craters will appear as your marbles crash and disturb your 'soil'.

GLOSSARY

asteroids Small, rocky objects that orbit the Sun, mostly in a region between the orbits of Mars and Jupiter known as the Asteroid Belt.

astronomer A scientist who studies the stars, planets, and other natural objects in space.

auroras Particles from the Sun that collide with the Earth's upper atmosphere, creating flickering bands of light. They are also called polar lights, northern lights, or southern lights.

black hole A small region of space with such strong gravity that light cannot escape it.

centaur A mythical creature with the head, arms, and upper body of a man, and the body and legs of a horse.

comets Small bodies made of rock, dust, and ice, which orbit the Sun.

constellation An area of the sky containing a pattern of stars that was invented by humans.

coronal mass ejections (CMEs) Clouds of electrified gas released from the Sun's surface.

craters Bowl-shaped hollows in an object's crust, often created by an impact from space.

electrons Tiny particles of matter that are smaller than an atom and have a negative electrical charge.

exoplanets Planets that orbit a star outside our solar system.

fireballs Extremely bright meteors with long tails.

flares Sudden bursts of matter and energy from the Sun.

galaxy A large number of stars, gas, dust, and dark matter, held together by gravity.

gravity A force that attracts all objects toward one another. The strength of the force depends on the objects' masses.

helium A very light substance, which is a gas at all but the lowest temperatures.

hemisphere Half of a sphere, such as a planet.

hydrogen A colorless gas that is the lightest and most common element in the Universe.

International Space Station (ISS) An orbiting space station involving five space programs and fifteen countries for scientific and space research.

interstellar Among the stars.

iron oxide A compound of oxygen and iron.

light-year The distance light travels in one year, a unit used to measure distances in astronomy.

lunar eclipse An occasion when the Earth is between the Sun and the Moon, so that the Moon passes into the Earth's shadow.

magnetic field An area surrounding a moving electric charge, or a magnet that produces pushes and pulls on other magnets, charges, and other objects.

mass A measure of the amount of matter in an object. In a gravitational field, the more mass an object has, the heavier (weightier) it is.

meteor The trail of light in the sky caused by a piece of rock or metal falling from space and burning up in Earth's atmosphere.

nebula A cloud of gas and dust in space.

neutron star A dead star in which the gravity is so high that its protons and electrons are crushed together and turn into neutrons.

orbit The path of one object around another in space, such as a planet around a star.

orrery A mechanical model of the solar system, in which the planets can be moved at the correct relative speeds around the Sun.

proton A particle with a positive electric charge found in the nuclei of all atoms.

red giant A dying star that is very big and bright.

red supergiant A dying monster star.

rover A wheeled robot that explores the surface of a planet, moon, or space object with a solid surface.

solar eclipse When the Moon passes directly in front of the Sun when viewed from Earth, and the Moon's shadow falls on Earth.

solar wind An eclipse of the Sun, when the Moon is between the Earth and the Sun so that for a short time, you cannot see part or all of the Sun.

stellar Relating to stars.

supernova A brilliant explosion that marks the death of some stars.

terminator The line that divides the sunlit part of the Moon from the dark part.

terrestrial Something that is made of or is on dry land, or relates to Earth.

waning Decreasing gradually in size, such as the decreasing visible portion of the Moon throughout each month.

waxing Increasing gradually in size, such as the increasing visible portion of the Moon throughout each month.

white dwarf The tiny but still hot and glowing core of a dead star.

FIND OUT MORE

Professor Raman Prinja, departmental head of Physics and Astronomy at University College London, is a preeminent astronomer and a multi-award-winning author of books that invite readers into the world of astronomy. He is an inspiring figure for children around the world and his passion for astrophysics is infectious as he spreads the joy of learning through events and community engagement.

Royal Observatory Greenwich in the UK is one of the most important sites in the world, and is the historic home of British astronomy, Greenwich Mean Time, and the Prime Meridian of the world. It was founded by Charles II in 1675 and now welcomes visitors and learners from around the globe.

Jan Bielecki is a Polish-Swedish illustrator and designer living in London. He mainly works with children's books and has illustrated fiction, picture books, and non-fiction. Some of the topics he has covered include the human anatomy, wrestling trolls, the scope of the universe and slimy monsters. He illustrated and designed Stephen and Lucy Hawking's *Unlocking the Universe*, as well as many of the most exciting covers put out by Puffin UK in recent years.

WEBSITES FOR THE SKY EXPLORER

Earth and Moon viewer:

www.fourmilab.ch/earthview

From this website you can view Earth, the Moon, and planets from different locations in the solar system. You can also view Venus, Mercury, and Mars, plus some moons. You can pretend to be at the Moon and see what Earth looks like from there!

Space weather:

www.spaceweather.com

Go here for updated, daily information on activity occurring on the Sun's surface, such as sunspots and flares. There are also aurorae alerts on this site; all part of the Sun-Earth connection we learnt about in this book!

Tonight's sky:

hubblesite.org/resource-gallery/learning-resources/tonights-sky

A rolling series of videos telling you which constellations are on view each month.

The planets today:

www.theplanetstoday.com

Take a look at where all the planets are in their orbits around the Sun today. You can even run the clock forward to see how their positions change.

Scale of the Universe:

scaleofuniverse.com

Here's your chance to explore and understand the vast size of the Universe. You can use a slide to move from Earth, across the solar system, and on to stars, galaxies, and the whole Universe.

For taking your astronomy further:

www.rmg.co.uk/royal-observatory

Check out Royal Observatory Greenwich's *Look Up!* podcast and *Night Sky Highlights* blog. Both are released monthly with exciting and clear guides to more treasures of the night sky.

www.youtube.com/c/RoyalObservatoryGrnwich

And don't forget their Astronomy at Home video playlist on YouTube for lots of engaging activities and other resources.

INDEX